CU00726434

JOHN
WESLEY
AT
WHITBY

With Some References
to National Events of the Times.

Compiled by

ALAN WHITWORTH

CULVA HOUSE PUBLICATIONS

First Published by Culva House Publications
in the year 2005

Culva House Publications • Whitby YO21 1RR
www.culvahouse.co.uk

© Alan Whitworth 2005

All rights reserved. No part of this publication
may be reproduced, stored in a retrieval system,
or transmitted in any form, or by any means
electronic, mechanical, photocopied, recorded
or otherwise, without the prior permission
of the publisher and copyright holder.

*With thanks to Bobbins, of Church Street, for the
loan of photographs of the former Wesleyan Chapel
and permission to reproduce them herein.*

ISBN 1 871150 50 7

Typeset in Baskerville Old Face
Typesetting and origination by
Culva House Publications

Printed and bound in Great Britain

JOHN WESLEY –
A BIOGRAPHICAL INTRODUCTION

John Wesley was born the fifteenth child of nineteen to Susanna (1669-1742) and Samuel Wesley (1662-1735) who were married in the year 1688. His father was known as the elder, having one of his children named Samuel. Samuel, the father, was a divine and poet, who originally spelt his name Westley. He was educated in London for Independent ministry between 1678 and 1683 on which date he entered Exeter College, Oxford. In 1685 he published a volume of verse entitled, *Maggots*. In 1688 Samuel gained an EA, and in 1694 a MA from Corpus Christi College, Cambridge, after which he became a naval chaplain, *c*.1689. He was rector of South Ormsby, 1690; then joint editor of *Athenian Gazette*, 1691-1697.

In 1695 Samuel Wesley became rector of Epworth, in Lincolnshire, and it was here that John was born; Samuel also held jointly the rectorship of Wroot, from 1722 until his death in 1735. He was involved in pecuniary difficulties by various accidents, and it is said his rectory was troubled by a noisy 'spirit' between the years 1716 and 1717. Later he published much verse and prose, including a panegyric on *Marlborough* (1705) and a hostile criticism of Nonconformist academies (1703); his dissertation on the Book of Job was published posthumously in 1735.

It was his mother Susanna, however, who was undoubtedly the biggest influence on her children's religious upbringing. She herself was one of three survivors of the twenty-four children of Samuel Annesley, a dissenting London minister. She had become an Anglican at the age of thirteen but never lost her Puritan heritage of serious devotion to spiritual and practical responsibilities. She kept a spiritual journal, read widely in theology, ran a disciplined and obedient household, and gave her children six hours' instruction a day in reading and writing from the age of five.

John Wesley, her fifteenth child (out of 19) and second surviving son, was prepared for Confirmation when he was eight. She was always concerned for his spiritual welfare, and he in his turn, felt able in his early ministry to consult her on theological questions. Charles Wesley, the other son, is best remembered as the author of over 5,500 hymns, but it was John who was his mother's favourite, exacerbated by an incident that occurred when he was six and fire destroyed the family home in the old Rectory at Epworth. At the very last moment, before the blazing thatch of the roof collapsed, young John was saved through an upstairs window. His mother felt that he had been marked out from her family as destined for great things – 'a brand, plucked from the burning'.

When Samuel her husband was away, she supplemented what she considered the curate's meagre spiritual offerings by holding informal kitchen meetings on Sunday evenings. They were intended for family and servants but attracted, audiences of over 200.

It is said that when Susanna wanted peace to pray in

her busy household, she simply pulled her apron over her head so that the children knew she was not to be disturbed.

Wesley left the fenland wastes of his village around 1714 for school in London, at the old Charterhouse. In 1720 John passed from the Charterhouse to Christ Church College, Oxford. He was ordained deacon in 1725. In 1726 he became a Fellow of Lincoln College and Greek lecturer there. In 1728 Wesley was ordained a priest in the Church of England. In 1727 he left Oxford briefly with the intentions of assisting his father, but returned as tutor in 1729. At this time he was much influenced by the spiritual writings of William Law (1686-1761). John became leader of a small dedicated group which had gathered round his brother Charles, nicknamed the 'Holy Club' or the 'Oxford Methodists', a name later adopted by Wesley for the adherents of the great evangelical movement that was its outgrowth. The members of the Society, who in 1730 were joined by James Hervey and George Whitefield (1714-1770), practised their religion with a then extraordinary degree of devotion, in strict accordance with the rubrics.

On his father's death in 1735, accompanied by his brother, John was appointed minister to the Colonists in Georgia, USA, and the two set sail from Gravesend in the *Simmonds*. Unfortunately, his lack of experience led the Rev. Wesley to make many mistakes and arouse the hostility of the community. After an unfortunate love-affair with a Miss Hopkey and under threat of a libel action, alone Wesley returned to England in 1738.

John had been influenced by Moravians on the voyage out, and on his return he met Peter Böhler, and attended 'society' meetings at Fetter Lane Chapel, London, as a member. At another meeting held in a house in Aldersgate Street, London, during the reading of Luther's preface to the Epistle to the Romans, he experienced an assurance of salvation which convinced him that he must bring the same assurance to others. But his unwonted zeal alarmed and angered most of the parish clergy, who closed their pulpits against him; this intolerance, and following Whitefield's example, he began preaching in the open air starting at Bristol in 1739. There he founded the first Methodist chapel. Later, he preached in, and bought, the ruinous gun-foundry at Moorfields, London, which was for many years the headquarters of Methodism in the capital. In the year 1740 he renounced Calvinism in his published 'free grace' sermons. Yet despite his continual brushes with the Established Church, so popular did he become that during his itinerary of half a century, often between 10,000 to 30,000 people would wait patiently for hours to hear him. He gave his strength to working-class neighbourhoods; hence the mass of his converts were colliers, miners, foundrymen, weavers and day-labourers in towns.

Wesley broke with the Moravians in 1745, and his acceptance of what was then known as an Arminian theology led to divergences with George Whitefield in 1741, a separate organisation of Calvinistic Methodists under the Countess of Huntingdon, and to an acute controversy with Augustus M. Toplady (1740-1778), author of that most famous hymn *Rock of Ages*.

Unlucky in love again, he became contracted to Grace Murray, a widow, in 1748 but assented to her marriage to John Bennett the following year. In 1751 he married the widow Mary Vazeille, but they had a serious disagreement in 1775, and she deserted him in 1776.

His life was frequently in danger, but he outlived all persecution, and the itineraries of his old age beginning in 1743 were triumphal processions from one end of the country to the other. His evangelistic journeys included visits to the Isle of Man, forty-two visits to Ireland (from 1747) and Scotland constantly (from 1751). During his unparalleled apostolate he travelled 225,000 miles and preached 40,000 sermons, his last being on 23 February 1791 the year of his death. His journeys and spiritual odyssey were recorded in his much published and renowned *Journal*.

John Wesley also managed to undertake a prodigious amount of other literary work, and produced grammars, extracts from the classics, histories, abridged biographies, twenty-three collections of psalms, hymns and tunes (1737 -1786), and prose under the title *Works* (1771-1774), and he founded the *Methodist Magazine* (1778). His writings were so popular that he made upward of £30,000, which he distributed in charity during his life. He also found time to set up charitable institutions at Newcastle and London, and established Kingswood School in Bristol.

Despite his differences Wesley nevertheless, was determined to remain loyal to the Church of England and urged his followers to do the same; "I live, and will die, a member of the Church of England," he always avowed; but increasing pressures were brought to bear on him and in 1784 he himself ordained one of his assistants (Francis Asbury) for work in the USA (much to his brother's distress), a practice which he later extended – this act many saw as Methodism separating from the Church of England. However, he always regarded Methodism as a movement within the Established Church and it remained so during his lifetime in this country.

In 1700 King William ruled a country of small communities which were fed largely by local labour on local farms. A century later King George III still ruled an agricultural kingdom, but one in which had appeared new sources of prosperity and wealth. Linked largely with the coalfields and London, steam power was taking over as the driving force behind the new enterprises. Men, women and children were summoned daily to the mills to tend the iron machines that spun yarn for cloth. Mines and quarries produced the coal, metal ores and clays which were needed in the towns. Raw materials and finished goods were transported not only by pack animals, but by the new canal system beginning to connect industrial areas.

Some old villages prospered from the workshops and small factories within them. They attracted people from the surrounding countryside who were anxious to find a better life than the precarious one on the farm; towns grew from this population movement, but the immigrant people were often poorly provided for, frequently without the support of nearby parish churches, too small or narrow-minded to cope with the rising populations – it was this background that enabled itinerant evangelists to preach and develop; new groups of people with 'Wesleyan' beliefs took hold, established their own churches and chapels, and as a consequence Methodism took a firm root in the land and spread with the travels of John Wesley, the founder of the movement.

FIRST VISIT TO WHITBY, 23 JUNE 1761

Although nearly 250 years have elapsed since the popular founder of Methodism first placed his earnest appeals before the crowds of Whitby, it cannot for a moment be supposed that the influence of his sincere teaching has vanished from this Eskside town.

On 23 June 1761, his day began at five o'clock in the morning, when John Wesley preached in the open air in the North Riding town of Guisborough. As soon as this very early service was completed he mounted his horse, faced the sun, and rode off in an easterly direction. He quickly discovered the ride to be of an exhausting nature, because of the intense heat prevailing that June morning. Luckily for him, this strain upon his endurance did not last long, for he writes:– "About eight the wind shifted, and, blowing in my face, made the journey much more agreeable." It must be borne in mind that when this agile equestrian made his first ride into Whitby, he was endowed with marvellous physical strength. At that date Wesley was fifty-six years of age.

The two special ideals of the incoming visitor lay in publishing Scripture truths as they revealed themselves to his own eager soul, and in leaving no corner of vice unreproved. Welcomed on his arrival by a goodly band of the kindly residents of the port, the indefatigable minister held forth again in the open air at six o'clock in the evening to the large congregation of Whitby shopkeepers, farmers, sailors and fishermen which had climbed to the top of the hill to hear the stranger's voice. Two decisive entries in his much-quoted *Journal* prove that the eloquent speaker faced the West Cliff from some eminence near the old church. "The sun shone on my face," he writes, "and the hill where I stood was ascended by 191 steps." The peaceful manner and the attentive hearing of ninety-nine percent of the crowd, earned the sincere gratitude and commendation of the fervent preacher. Later still, Wesley held a meeting "with his own Society." Subsequently, he conversed with one of his lady adherents. He writes that she "was a very sensible woman." Needless to say, their conversation turned upon important topics of theology and the lady's opinion coincided with his own.

Very much alive to the natural attractions and historic buildings of the numerous towns he passed through, Wesley inspected St. Hilda's Abbey on the Wednesday, and wrote: "I walked round the old Abbey, which, both with regard to its size (being, I judge, one hundred yards long) and the workmanship of it, one of the finest, if not the finest ruin in the kingdom." It should be noted here at that period St. Hilda's ruins possessed far larger dimension than now. Two years after Wesley's visit the west side of the nave fell, and in 1830 the high central tower came down.

While this was Wesley's first visit to Whitby, it was not his first excursion to the district. In July 1757, he had preached from the quay of Robin Hood's Bay. It was in the reign of King George III when he first appeared in the

tiny hamlet, and it was this monarch who remained on the throne throughout the eleven visits of John Wesley to this ancient seaport.

How did England fare in 1761? These were turbulent times. In the very month when Wesley's pen described Whitby's venerable ruin, an English army, sent abroad by the elder William Pitt (1708-1778), Secretary of State, gained considerable victories over the Gallic foes. However, a sad disaster lay in store for England, when this truly magnificent statesman laid down the reigns of his exalted office four months later. At that period, along the current of the winding Esk, did Tories and Whigs ever pass from noisy crowds to violent blows? Undoubtedly, among the large congregation which assembled to hear the words of one who shared with Whitefield the title of England's most popular Evangelist, the followers of both Pitt and Charles J. Fox (1749-1806) could be found.

SECOND VISIT, 19 APRIL 1764

Three years later Wesley awoke in Scarborough on the morning of April 19th. At the early hour of five o'clock he held a final meeting with his friends there, which he called his 'parting blessing'. He then mounted horse and rode northwards, making his beast climb up and down the steep hills which bar the southern approaches to Robin Hood's Bay. On his second visit to this quaint seaside village, at two o'clock in the afternoon, he preached in the little square to an open air and orderly crowd. He remarks, "A poor mad-man came, but sat down quietly until the sermon ended." Resuming his journey Wesley rode the final six

Whitby harbour, looking towards Wesleyan Chapel.

Wesley Chapel, Church Street opened by Rev. John Wesley, 1788.

miles before descending into the picturesque valley wherein Whitby lies.

During the intervening years from his first to this his second visit, a meeting house had either been erected or purchased. Wesley preached in it at six o'clock, but he declared "it ill contained the congregation." Nevertheless, the visitor duly and thankfully acknowledged the progressive growth of the Whitby Society.

On the Saturday, Wesley called upon a bereaved widow who "lay ill in bed." The sacred book tells of Rachel weeping for her children; ancient mythology gives the lamentable story of the slain children of Niobe; but somehow this sorely stricken Whitby mother excels them, rivalling Chaucer's Griselde in her inexhaustible fund of patience. She had buried seven of her family in six months, and her 'beloved husband and just been cast away at sea.' The preacher enquired, "Do you not fret at any of these things?" With a lovely smile on her pale cheek the invalid answered, "How can I fret at anything which is the will of God? He has given me Himself; I love, I praise Him every moment." Her thanksgiving and resignation astonished Wesley. Truly this Whitby lady had placed her feet upon Bunyan's land of Beulah. The next day, Easter Sunday, became a red letter day in the religious history of this ancient port. Wesley sums up his day's work thus: "I preached in the Room at five and eight. There was such a number of communicants at church as it was supposed had not been there for fifty years. In the evening, I preached under the cliff, for the sake of those who were not able to get up the hill. The skirts of the congregation could not hear, though my voice was clear and loud; but the bulk of them seemed to hear and understand. How ripe for God is this place?" This master of glowing speech did not tarry in Whitby, however, although the pleasure and advantage of seeing the town at its best in such a lovely spring was his.

On Monday morning the assiduous visitor preached at five o'clock, and met his select Society, declaring himself "well pleased with it." Riding west, he preached before he retired that day at Stokesley, in Gusiborough and Hutton Rudby: a notable achievement, four sermons in four different places in one day, and a long hilly country ride between each. This is how Wesley contrived to deliver eight hundred sermons in a year.

On Tuesday, he occupied the pulpit in what he calls "the new House at Yarm." He admires the work of the architect, asserting this house "to be by far the most elegant in England." An enquiry forces itself upon our minds: were the Yarm Wesleyans richer or more generous than their co-religionists? Whitby then formed part of the Yarm Circuit – a Circuit which numbered 825 members in the year 1766. Was it possible the wealth had travelled inland to fund this palace of high ideals?

Whitefield and the two Wesley's did not adopt the fashion of the Old Testament Nazarites; leaving the triviality of whether one house was better than another, what was the burning question which upset the pacific equilibrium of the residents of the Capital? Nowadays the Premier and Lord Mayor work amicably, however, in those times these high authorities were at daggers drawn. Rightly or wrongly, John Wilkes (1727-1797) made severe onslaughts on the unpopular Ministers of the Crown; and possibly because of this rightly or wrongly, he became the

idol of the populace. It was in this year England sustained a deep loss in the death of the inimitable William Hogarth (1697-1764), satirical cartoonist, who did much to show the world the absurdities of society and political life in the eighteenth century.

THIRD VISIT, 11 JULY 1766

After spending two more years in colossal travelling, writing and speaking, John Wesley decided a third time to visit the narrow lanes and streets of Whitby. He beheld this section of the Yorkshire coast once in April, eight times in June, and twice in July. Never did his eyes rest upon it when wearing its winter garb of snow and ice or wrapped in the fogs of November. Rising with the lark on Friday, 11 July 1766, the active preacher again sermonised to four sets of hearers. Waking in Hutton Rudby, he began his first public service there at the usual five o'clock. Proceeding in the direction of Stokesley, he preached in the new chapel of that town. Later still, taking a north-easterly ride, he entered Guisborough and gave his third sermon. Pushing forward two miles to the East Coast, the eloquent equestrian wound up his long day of physical, mental and spiritual toil by proclaiming his fourth and last Gospel message in Whitby. Yet the endurance and stability of his vocal powers remained intact, enabling their possessor to write: "I was no more tired than when I woke in the morning."

Resting these four July days in some Whitby home – we wish we could learn whose residence gave welcome hospitality and who's stable took the preachers steed – the

Rev. Wesley is silent concerning his Saturday plans and purposes, yet a scholar knows no ennui, writing as he did thirty or forty letters per week, and his correspondence took up much time. Moreover, during the year, he brought out a theological work of 162 pages. Probably too, during this long summer's day, the picturesque attractions of his surroundings held captive his keen and enquiring mind which took an interest in everything around him both natural and scientific.

Zealously toiling on Sunday, his *Journal* reveals: "I preached at seven in the Room, and at one in the main street at the other side of the water. A vast multitude ran together (see page 13) and was deeply attentive. At five, I preached in the New Market Place to a still larger congergation." Bossuet, the sublime French orator, had continually on his lips the words, "Let this Scared Book never leave your hands." Similarly Wesley cried, "Be a man of the Book." A very homely proverb says, 'The early bird catches the worm.' There were in the eighteenth century Whitby people who gave credence to such a wise adage. Hence, at five o'clock on Monday morning, a number of early risers witnessed the departure of their reverend leader. Wesley avers, "They had a solemn parting," ere he mounted his horse en route for Robin Hood's Bay.

Remembering the early hours in which these Wesleyans met, we affirm that Solomon's drastic admonition, 'Go to the ant, thou sluggard,' would have been superfluous in Whitby. Such prompt dwellers in ancient Streonshalh needed no Daylight Saving Bill; they were ready for the fatigues of a long day without any interference from a fussy House of Commons. At the very time when the farmers of Robin Hood's Bay were carting their sweet-scented newly mown hay, just now when Wesley gripped so tenaciously the North Riding fishermen, George III exercised his kingly prerogative and dismissed Rockingham from the position of head of the Ministry. Yes in this very month, the aforesaid monarch called upon Pitt to become Prime Minister, creating him Earl of Chatham. Alas for England, her new Premier suffered from a serious mental disturbance that kept him away from Parliamentary duties. We may take it as a piece of fathomless irony, that the talented demagogue John Wilkes received more applause in the streets of London than either Pitt or Wesley – the cry of Wilkes and Liberty may have stirred the hearts of some of the Sandsend Alum workers suffering under the yoke of their masters. Eleven years later Whitby owned 251 ships; twelve or thirteen of them sailed northwards for whale fishing in Greenland. Possibly some of them carried into the Arctic regions the hymns and sayings of the Wesley brothers.

FORTH VISIT, 15 JUNE 1770

Four years elapsed when Wesley, finding himself in the market town of Thirsk, decided on a fourth visit to this seaport. First of all he guided his horse in a northerly direction to Stokesley. He also desired to mend the ways of his countrymen in more senses than one, hence he writes: "The whole road from Thirsk to Stokesley, which used to be extremely bad, I found better than most turnpikes." Turning to the east, the much-travelled equestrian rode on to the shores of the North Sea.

The familiar figure of John Wesley on horseback,
often seen reading a book as he rode about the countryside

Reaching his destination, having already delivered fifteen sermons in five days, he thought of preaching quietly in the Room but discovering his seaside friends had advertised an open air service, he proceeded to the Whitby Market Place. The congregation listened well, and is described in his *Journal* as 'deeply attentive' to the captivating words of the reverend speaker.

17

It is on this visit that one of the difficult dilemmas of leadership thrust itself before Wesley on the 16th day of June. The Rev. James Brownfield, an itinerant of six years standing, had withdrawn and set up for himself at Whitby. However, Mr. Brownfield appears to have been a very determined and controversial Nonconformist and it seems that Wesley was faced with the prospect of trying to bring the clerical gentleman back into the fold, or at least to reason with him over some matters of which no record survives except Wesley's intentions to talk with him. How we wish we were privy to the conclusion of their discourse. Saturday afternoon Wesley set aside for literary work. He examined Dr. Priestley's *English Grammar*, and wondered whether "he should publish it after Bishop Lowth's."

On Sunday, early in the morning, he met the Select Class of sixty-five. At 8am he preached and at nine o'clock he held a children's service. Later, he became a hearer attending the morning service of Mr. Brownfield, where he heard "a poor sermon." Wesley pithily remarks, "However, I went again in the afternoon, remembering the words of Philip Henry, 'If the preacher does not know his duty, I know mine.' Yet it is easy to be too critical; one cannot always expect to listen to pulpit eloquence rivalling that of a Florentine Savonarola, or an English Whitefield! Moreover, in pulpit oratory as well as platform eloquence Wesley did not say with our Continental neighbours, *Chacun à son goût*. Between one and two, Wesley met the Bands of his Society; at five he preached in the open Market Place to a greater congregation than before. Later still, he conducted a love feast of two hours' duration.

Finally, at nine o'clock he met the children, "most of whom had known the way of God." What a fine record of achievement; what a healthy throat the preacher possessed. Ever vigorous, next day at noon, he proclaims his message to the fisher folk of Robin Hood's Bay as he left the area.

It was not just in the North, but everywhere that a strange and intense longing to hear this master of popular diction took hold. In London, for instance, John Wesley was announced to preach at George Whitefield's funeral sermon in Moorfields four months after this visit to Whitby in 1770. The time appointed was 5.30pm. The Tabernacle was crowded at three, so the preacher commenced an hour-and-a-half before the time and still ran to his allotted span.

FIFTH VISIT, 19 JUNE 1772

Two more years elapsed before Wesley decided to make a fifth and brief sojourn where the white seagulls of Whitby pursue their swimming prey in the tidal harbour of the Esk. On 19th June he preached at eight o'clock in the morning at Stokesley.

Appealing to his own *Journal*, we find the author writing: "I crept over the moors to Castleton. The congergation was gathered for many miles around. It was with much difficulty we got from hence to Whitby between six and seven." Specially mark that plural pronoun 'we'. The Rev. L. Tyreman writes: "Mrs. Wesley accompanied her husband in a chaise on his fifth visit." Under such conditions, over steep hills that lie between Castleton and Whitby, the journey in a chaise was compelled to be accomplished with a greater expenditure of time and with more difficulty than on horseback the roads being in a poor state. Coming down into Whitby and staying there on the Friday and Saturday evenings, can anyone say in whose dining room Mr. and Mrs. Wesley partook of refreshment, and in whose bedroom they slept? The rough journey completed, the reverend visitor met and was cheered by forty members of his lively Society, so the day ended pleasantly.

Wesley many a time and oft had crossed the Whitby moors and Scarborough hills safely, meeting with no untoward circumstances. In other parts of the kingdom, however, unpleasant adventures befell the rider in his innumerable equestrian journeys. Sometimes he rode as many as ninety miles in a single day. A horse fell dead under his saddle near Bristol. Riding in Southwark, Wesley's steed came down and pinned the rider beneath, crushing his ankle, and compelling him to lay up for a brief period. Sometimes disasters, however, proved a blessing in disguise. Soon after this accident, a generous lady, a Miss Margaret Leaven, of Durham, made the itinerant preacher a present of a chaise and a pair of horses – a very welcome present to any gentlemen who finds himself in the seventh decade of his life as Wesley was at this date.

Henceforth he took to driving in a chaise, and rarely appeared as the familiar equestrian. Moreover, this chaise was fitted with shelves, and they carried some of his favourite books. He began to suffer from hydrocele, but neither age, nor pain, nor persecution could damp the ardour of this shepherd in his desire to benefit his Whitby

A woodcut view of Whitby Parish Church as it appeared in Thomas Gents, History of Hull, 1735.

flock. Saturday, on a fair, mild evening in this leafy month of June, he preached "on the smooth green top of the hill just above the Church." Only once during his eleven visits was an unseemly and vindictive attempt made to drown his voice. His *Journal* records: "Saturday, 20th.— As soon as I began to preach, some men began ringing the bells; but it was lost labour, for all the people could hear to the very skirts of the congregation."

It is not known whether Mr. and Mrs. Wesley spent the Sunday night in Whitby or Robin Hood's Bay. From either coign of vantage they, during the long days of summer, could discern bright seascapes with white foaming billows. The inhabitants of the latter seaport gathered to hear this master of assemblies at noon. Subsequently, in their chaise, the couple journeyed over the southern hills into Scarborough.

How distinctly the minds of men are cast into different moulds. How greatly the temperaments of the sons of Adam differ, and how various the results that arrive. Some develop a personal magnetism which ever anon draws men to their side – magnetism which tends to make their fellow men subservient to their wills. Others grow up under the influence of a repelling planet. The latter drive men away; even when they perform a generous action they do it at the wrong moment, and they spoil it by their frigid manner. Wesley belonged to the former class; Lord Frederick North (1732-1792) to the latter. Have we not at far-distant intervals suffered from domineering Statesmen, who, careless of public manifestations, never felt where the national shoe pinched until too late? In spite of all pro-tests, Lord North persevered in taxing tea imported by the American colonists. *Hinc illæ lachrymor.* Ever blind to facts, obdurate in temper, this unlucky Premier brought overwhelming disasters upon his native land. *Cui bono?*

When the indignation of our trans-Atlantic brethren grew by leaps and bounds, there was the cool statement, "Their lawlessness"; but in the Far West they dubbed it "sane patriotism." George III and his chief Minister lacked the penetrating foresight so well displayed in Shake-speare's keen adage, 'A little fire is quickly trodden out, which, being suffered, rivers cannot quench.' In the New World, British officers and tax-gatherers received continual insults.

In this very year, a few bold spirits of the Paul Revere type, boarded, captured and burnt the English ship of war, *HMS Gasparee*. What a striking contrast – Wesley quietly expounding Holy Writ, whilst the waves broke peacefully on the Whitby Strand, and excited Colonists cheered frantically as the blazing embers of the doomed ship fell, splashing the waters of the Atlantic! Dressed with a little brief authority, how easily do modern members of Parliament impose new taxes accompanied by irritating regulations. Possessing no claims to infallibility, the Whitby Evangelist hit the right nail on the head before the great War of Independence started off. He wrote to Lord North, putting these pertinent enquiries:– "Is it common sense to use force against the Americans? These men will not be frightened. They will probably dispute every inch of the ground. They want nothing but a leader. Remember Charles the First."

SIXTH VISIT, 1 JULY 1774

With indefatigable zeal, the extensively travelled founder of the Methodist Movement paid a sixth visit on July 1st 1774. On Friday morning, his public worship began at Stokesley. From that hilly place, he went on twelve miles to Guisborough and held another service there. In the afternoon he crossed over the steep hills which lie between Gusiborough and the North Sea. Wesley's activities began on the Sunday morning at five o'clock by meeting the Society. At eight, he discoursed on the warning text, "How shall we escape if we neglect so great a salvation?" At the usual hour, he attended the morning service at Church. During the time Wesley sat as a hearer inside, a tragic accident happened outside. A fearless man diverted himself by swimming . . . but unfortunately, he miscalculated his strength, for Wesley writes, "he sunk and rose no more." The *Journal* contains this sentence: "The minister preached in the afternoon a sermon suited for the occasion; 'Be ye also ready, for ye know not when the Son of Man cometh.'

On the familiar site of the Market Place (opposite), at five o'clock in the afternoon, Wesley's persuasive voice rang out the praises of charity. The text selected was 1 Corinthians xiii, 1. At that date, urgent necessity existed for such a homily. The orator, both by his voice and pen, contended for a more compassionate treatment of the poor, of lunatics, and of convicted criminals. The Draconian laws against which Wesley inveighed not only treated men with awful severity, but women especially with almost unspeakable barbarity. What could the Christian men and women of Whitby say to an item like this: 'In 1767, Ann Sowerby was burnt at York for murdering her dreadful husband?'

Ever devoted to his ministry, at 11 o'clock we find Wesley unfolding the treasures of the scriptures to a crowd in the Square at Robin Hood's Bay. Pressing southwards he gets hold of a numerous assembly "in the new House at Scarborough." He differentiates between his hearers there and those at Bridlington: of the Scarborough Chapel he writes :– "One of the neatest and most elegant preaching houses in England. Now let the people walk worthy of their calling, and there will be good work in this place."

On the Wednesday evening, Wesley did not seem to get a hold of the crowd, for he says: "At Bridlington-Key, I preached to as stupid and ill-mannered a congregation as I have seen for many years."

Nationally, Lord North kept on wrangling with the Americans and professing to tax them. Scolding these Congress men was as profitable as howling at the moon. The fiery eloquence of Chatham, Edmund Burke (1729-97), and Fox pleaded their cause in vain. Our trans-Atlantic brethren resolved to appeal to Mars the God of arms. Wesley, ever ready to denounce oppression, printed a pamphlet, *Thoughts on Slavery*. Tyreman tells us that a "Philadelphian gentleman republished in America Wesley's tract." Both as an author and preacher Wesley's words were within reach of Whitby readers and listeners.

SEVENTH VISIT, 20 JUNE 1779

Writing in 1779, Lionel Charlton in his *History* says; 'Mr. Wesley annually visits Whitby'. This is a slight exaggeration. Although this persuasive organiser wrote, "Leisure and I have shaken hands and parted company," yet he could only call upon his Whitby brothers eleven times in a period of thirty years. Between the sixth and seventh visits, five years passed, and then Wesley made another brief entry into ancient Streonshalh.

A most oppressive heat wave passed over England at that time. Wesley had spent two summers in Savannah, and had had experience of the American climate; still he holds the opinion that just now eighteen or twenty days "were as hot as in Georgia." One of the most pleasing episodes of his arduous life occurred before this seventh visit. In Newcastle-upon-Tyne he received a most cordial welcome in the home of his step-daughter, Mrs. Smith. Her gracious hospitality led her step-father to chronicle his regret at leaving "such a lovely place and such lovely company." Ten years later, when making his will, the grateful guest remembered his "dear grand-daughters, Mary and Jane Smith."

On Saturday, 26th June after giving two congregations the benefit of his religious teaching, the self-denying preacher saw again the venerable ruins of Whitby Abbey. The entry in his *Journal* for this sojourn reads: "Saturday, I went on to our loving, earnest brethren at Whitby. Sunday, 27th, I preached at eight in the Room, and at five in the Market Place to a huge congregation. They were no more deeply affected than the stones they stood upon." In this cryptic comment Wesley refers to the latter listeners. Did the intense heat render the preacher careless of the effects of the sun on his congregation standing there for up to two hours, or where the crowd really inattentive?

The aforesaid Room at that date was an octagonal building near to the sea, in Henrietta Street. It had for fifteen years been used for Divine worship by the first Whitby Wesleyans, and was said to be one of the largest buildings in the country.

This seventh visit at Whitby formed part of a tour all along the East Coast as usual. On the Monday, he travelled along the elevated road to Robin Hood's Bay (*see* Map Page 46) and Scarborough, and at both seaside places his voice pleaded for righteous and consecrated lives.

Previously, at odd intervals for a quarter of a century,

in the quaint fishing village of Robin Hood's Bay, he had proclaimed his scriptural message in the open air, and generally about midday. Now he had over his head another roof beside the blue dome of heaven, for on the 28th June 1779 he writes: "I preached in the new preaching house in Robin Hood's Bay" Ever a diligent student of facts and an omnivorous reader, Wesley got hold of an perused a copy of Charlton's *A History of Whitby*, which he said contained "curious things."

We joyfully note, on his way to Bridlington, the busy itinerant spared an hour or two to inspect the bold promontory of Flamborough Head. Of it he writes: "It is a huge rock rising perpendicular from the water to an immense height, which gives shelter to innumerable multitude of sea-fowl of various kinds."

Bridlington this year endured the agony of witnessing the arrival of a very different and forcible character – John Paul Jones, naval adventurer, who engaged and captured two British war vessels in sight of Flamborough Head. In the hotly contested battle Jones obtained victory, but had 300 of his men slain.

Whilst Wesley carried on his usual pious labours England suffered some terrible tribulations. Pitt's great genius unemployed; Washington commanding revolting Colonists; France and Spain declare war against the country; Gibraltar closely besieged, and Warren Hastings fighting Mahrattas in India. After our troops had taken up arms, Wesley loyally supported the Government of the day. As may be expected, this change of front incurred the deep anger of the Colonists in view of his earlier stance. Detesting from their very soul his backing of England's military proceedings, indignant Americans nevertheless considered Wesleyan doctrines attractive and worthy of adoption; and the total number of membership rose to 7,328,829 about that date. Wesley would have been well advised if he had left the Independence question alone. He had written so convincingly against the taxation of the Colonies as to make other utterances void of real effect.

On this side of the Atlantic, Wesley continued with his endeavours as normal, among which involved the enrolment of a deed of Chancery on 28th February, appending to it the names of his chief supporters which include the names of two Whitby gentlemen – Robert Hopkins and William Thom.

EIGHTH VISIT, 6 JUNE 1784

Now an octogenarian, the amount of vigour and oratorical power he still possessed, astonished everyone. Almost a stranger to fatigue, yet wanting only twelve days to complete his eight-first year, Wesley again descended the declivities that enclosed Whitby. On Wednesday, 17th June, the third sermon of that day from his lips was delivered to the Whitby crowds. The next morning, the House filled to listen to his preaching. That Thursday his vigilant eye scanned the habiliments of his feminine congregation with distinct approval. He alludes to their piety and demure in these words: "The Society here may be a pattern to all England. They despise all ornaments but good works, together with a meek and quiet spirit. I did not see a ruffle, no, nor a fashionable cap among them; though many of them were in easy circumstances." In the evening Wesley sallied forth to the oft-used Market Place, and addressed a crowd that "would have filled the House three times over."

On the Friday we are not privy to his movements, nor the Saturday; and he adopted the usual course of not spending his Sabbath in the town. In the morning after the usual five o'clock service and departure he took the road to Robin Hood's Bay, and notes a greater harmony in that congregation, and in the evening the Scarborough people heard his prompt and clear elocution.

This year Samuel Johnson died (*b*.1709); he had written and spoken very kindly of Wesley. They had met and conversed together in London. The leviathan had written of the preacher: "I love his pious zeal." Whitby, as elsewhere, reaped the toil of this great Lexicographer. An excited General Election in 1784 gave a large majority to Pitt and placed him firmly on the saddle of government. Pitt and Fox where then the highest names in the political controversies of the day.

NINTH VISIT, 13 JUNE 1786

Only four days from his eighty-fourth birthday, Wesley decided to make his ninth visit to Whitby, which visit turned out to be the last to the old meeting House in Henrietta Street. His long and earnest life had now enabled him to outlive all manner of violence, persecution and slander. No long was he subjected to scenes such as had occurred in his earlier life and in such places as Halifax. Here, for instance, on one visit in the year 1748 Wesley attempted to preach at the cross in the middle of the Old

Market, which caused a great commotion in the town. Wesley wrote: "There was an immense number of people roaring like the waves of the sea, but the far greater part of them were still, and as soon as I began to speak they seemed more and more attentive." To break up the meeting, it is recorded in other sources that a gentleman 'scutched' half-pennies among the crowd; then there was confusion, in which stones and mud were flung at the preacher. A few days later Wesley was mobbed at Colne, and he retired to Widdop, from which safe refuge, he wrote a letter of remonstrance to the Church Minister of Colne, who had encouraged the rioters.

Wesley was again at Widdop, in the Calder Valley, in 1766, and the rock from which he preached is still known as Wesley's Pulpit.

The new Wesleyan Chapel, Halifax, in the 19th century.

The formation of rocks known as Wesley's Pulpit, high on the moors above Widdop in the Calder Valley, in which region lies Halifax town; scenery reminiscent of the moors around Whitby.

The tide had indeed changed. Everywhere admiring crowds greeted his appearance. On Tuesday, 13th June 1786, his aged voice rang forth four times. Passing through Guisborough, he came across a crowd waiting as to induce him to halt and address them.

Notwithstanding the intense heat of the season, and the long uncomfortable journey, like the Apostle of the Gentiles he longed to look upon his followers with a paternal eye. "We had a warm ride in the afternoon to Whitby. In the evening the House was well filled with people and with the fear of God."

Wesley likewise mentions the virtue of a recently deceased Whitby gentleman, William Ripley, likening him to John the Baptist. By 1770 distinct differences had arisen in the Wesleyan ranks in Whitby, and the two factions centred on Messrs. Ripley and Brownfield as respective leaders. Eventually the latter and his friends chose to leave the congregation and as we have heard previously, Brownfield established and erected his own chapel in Silver Street. William Ripley for a long time then bore the heat and burden of the day of the Wesleyan Society, and Wesley paid due respect to the Christian qualities of this man.

John Wesley's *Journal is* reticent about the activities of Wednesday, but on Thursday his extensive talents were employed in Scarborough. His keen practical vision took in all worlds. Orator, linguist, author, he never posed as the ultra-refined dilettante gentleman, dedicated to nothing temporal. Time and again he restrained individuals from building more expensive chapels than they could pay for. He gave utilitarian advice over many mundane affairs; he strongly urged all men with property to make wills; he called upon all public speakers to use clear language; he invited gentlemen afflicted with lowness of spirit to take an hour's exercise daily.

The popular entertainments of England sadly lacked compassion and refinement. Whitby in the North Riding may have been more merciful than Birstall in the West, where at the latter bull-baiting was still a popular spectator sport encouraged by the government throughout the eighteenth century, and in Halifax, the gibbet still plied its horrible trade for public amusement leading to the popular saying – From Hell, Hull and Halifax, Good Lord Preserve us!

TENTH VISIT, 13 JUNE 1788

The most remarkable of all the eleven visits paid by John Wesley to Whitby, must surely have been the tenth. On this occasion, joy and sorrow were co-mingled. Arriving from the hilly west, Wesley left his chaise, entered the pulpit, and preached the opening sermon of the New Chapel in Church Street, on 13th June 1788. What had become of the old Rooms? What had happened in the two year interval to the town? In the incessant warfare between sea and land so common along the Yorkshire coast, the stormy waves smash along the shore and headland in a ceaseless manner. The undermining of the cliff, erosion, caused a large portion of the headland to tumble into the sea, bringing down part of the street and causing the Methodist Chapel to come with it.

This district has been pointed out as the veritable site

*Two views of the collapse of Henrietta Street, in which the
Wesleyan Chapel so long in use, tumbled into the sea with a
number of other properties at Christmastime.*

35

of the ancient Streonshalh; the road through, before paving lay in a rough state of nature. Lionel Charlton gave it that it first bore the title 'Haglathe'. He tells us, "By degrees, it formed into a complete street, called Henrietta Street [after the wife of the Lord of the Manor]." Notwithstanding the proximity of the tide, the street gained in favour, until it was said to "have grown so populous that not less than 1,000 inhabitants are to be found in the same."

When the first Wesleyan Room fell into the waters, what business occupied the men and women to whom Wesley came with his searching appeals? Seven or eight hundred spinners and a number of weavers made canvas for the sails of ships; four hundred men and boys hammered away and built twenty-five vessels yearly; and 251 ships belonged to Whitby owners. Another great industry was the production of alum; as much as "6,000 tons were wrought" in a twelve-month period.

Wesley too, was not the first world-famous theologian to make an impact on the residents. George Fox (1624-1691) had brought his words to the town and there are said to have been three hundred members of the Society of Friends, certainly many eminent persons in business and commerce were adherents to the Quaker life and they had a sound meeting house and burial ground.

Two calamities reduced the numbers of living inhabitants at that period – Smallpox and destructive storms. Wesley in his *Journal* alludes to the former. Before the introduction of vaccinations, epidemics of this fatal kind augmented the number of burials in the old churchyard around St. Mary's church. Then again, when 4,000 sailors "went down to the sea in ships", how many found a watery grave when Neptune indulged in his fierce moods?

The New Chapel in which Wesley preached on this occasion was erected on a more commanding site, and held twice as much congregation as the vanished one. Its presence delighted the aged preacher. Many details appeared to him *couleur de rose*. However, one drawback at that date which concerned the venerable orator was the incomplete brick and joinery work.

"The unfinished galleries having as yet no fronts, were frightful to look upon. It is the most curious House we have in England. You go up to it by about forty steps, and then you have before you a lofty front, I judge over fifty feet high, and fifty-four feet broad. So much gainers have we been by the loss of the former House! Besides that it stood at one end of the town, and in the very sink of it, where people of fashion were ashamed to be seen."

Despite its state, Wesley was proud of its presence. With a huge assembly anticipated for Wesley's opening sermon, one precaution was taken. As the front of the galleries remained unfinished, strong men wishing to prevent accidents sat on the edge with their feet dangling over their friends below.

The next day, Saturday, the same *persona grata* occupied the pulpit. At five o'clock, and in the evening, two large congregations rewarded with gifts the labours of the builders of the New Chapel, and the preacher notes "the uncommon earnestness of the people." When Sunday morning dawned, "the old man, eloquent" with the incomprehensible fascination he wielded, filled the Chapel at seven o'clock. At half-past-one, he preached from the text 'The end of all things is at hand; be ye therefore sober

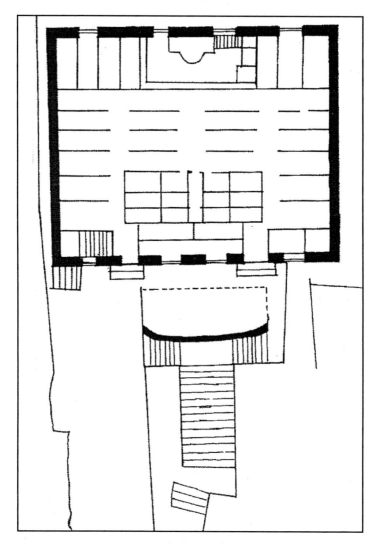

*A Ground Plan of the new Wesleyan Methodist Chapel,
off Church Street (at the Bottom) opened in 1788 by Wesley.*

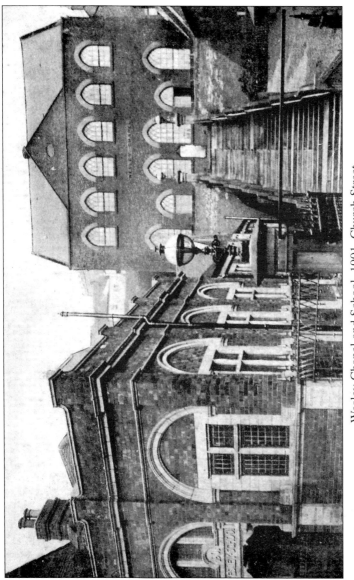

Wesley Chapel and School, 1901. Church Street.

Wesley's Pulpit, Church Street Wesleyan Chapel.

and watch and pray.' He undertook the afternoon service "for the sake of country people, who flocked in from all sides."

"For the sake of the country people," wrote the veteran minister. A learned divine published a statement suggesting that Wesley cared little for farmers and did not frequently preach where congregations were sparse and agricultural in nature. The *Journals*, however, refute this. At Foggathorpe, Rufforth, Poppleton, Sykehouse, Hutton Rudby, Easingwold, Tollerton, Osmotherley, and dozens of small places, Wesley did indeed spend his strength where the assemblies were sparse.

Ignoring weariness and old age, he preached again five in the afternoon, "and took up a collection for the Kingswood School, the rather that I might refute that poor, threadbare slander of my getting so much money." The worship of this first Sunday in the new Chapel concluded with a love-feast. A splendid achievement for a man just twelve days short of his eighty-fifth birthday, and still grieving the death of his brother Charles only a week or so before.

As far as we know, Charles Wesley never appeared in the narrow streets of Whitby, and his face and his form were unknown to the dwellers on the Esk. Yet tens of thousands of Christian men and women have sung, and will no doubt continue to sing such incomparable hymns as *Jesus Lover of My Soul*, *Hark the Herald Angels Sing*, and *Oh for a Heart to Praise my God*; and let no man forget it was Charles who began the Godly Club of Oxford Methodists from which sprang the movement. The Godly Club developed into the Class Meeting, which Whitefield and Wesley then transformed into Open Air meetings which it is known sometimes numbered as many as 10,000 souls in attendances.

FINAL VISIT TO WHITBY, 18 JUNE 1790

"The Pitcher that goes often to the well, comes home at last." It is calculated by Canon Overton, that Wesley after the age of thirty-six, travelled 225,000 miles, and preached more than 40,000 sermons. In an enfeebled condition, but still able to ride eighty miles in a coach, and preach the same day, the great orator beheld the charming and romantic scenery which surrounds Whitby for the last time.

During the previous year, diabetes, in an attack in Ireland, had reduced his strength. The veteran evangelist could not free himself from its weakening tendencies. Nevertheless, in scorn of any personal consequences, his soul yearned to meet his followers on Yorkshire's coast once more. On 13th June 1790, the congregation in Monk-wearmouth Church listened to his sermon, and then he made his farewells and on the 18th June he preached for the last time in the Chapel on Church Street. Honoured, obeyed, and loved, he spent Saturday and Sunday with his beloved Society in this ancient seaport. On his last Sabbath he preached twice, and attended the Chapel once. The *Journal* of 1790 records his affection for the town and that of the people for him. "It was very providential that part of the adjoining mountain fell down and demolished our old meeting House, with many houses besides by which means, we have one of the most beautiful chapels in

Great Britain, finely situated on the steep side of the mountain. In all England, I have not seen a more affecttionate people than those at Whitby." Alas that fine Chapel was demolished some years ago, only the steps and a fine red-brick Sunday School building survive, and the latter was erected centuries after the death of Wesley, who would have been proud to know that the movement still flourished here.

The following Sunday, Wesley spent in the important port of Hull. On Monday, 28th June, he celebrated his eighty-eight birthday in that commercial city. Even then, suffering from feeble eyesight he got through an amazing amount of business. The persevering philanthropist, John Howard, a native of that place, died in 1790. Of this generous Englishmen Wesley wrote: "I had the pleasure of conversation with Mr. Howard, I think one of the greatest men in Europe."

Nine months after bidding farewell to Whitby, Wesley gave his final sermon at Leatherhead, on 23rd February, 1791. The next day he wrote his last letter to the slave emancipator, William Wilberforce (1759-1833), of Hull. A little later drowsiness set in and finally, in his own bedroom in London, on 2nd March 1791, Wesley passed into the hands of death.

How long did it take the news of John Wesley's demise to reach the ears of his brethren in Whitby? How long did the congregation of the new Church Street Chapel grieve for their master and founder? Ancient Streonshalh can justly boast of its ecclesiastical ancestors and events that first put this seaport on the map – St. Hilda, Cædmon, and the great Synod of AD664 which settled the appointment of Easter Day; may not the town be also proud that such divine clerics as George Fox and John Wesley, also established themselves in the hearts and minds of those industrious fishermen and their families standing in that open Market Place nearly three centuries ago.

Whaling ships returning home to Whitby.

GENERAL INDEX

*Figures in **Bold** denote an illustration*

43

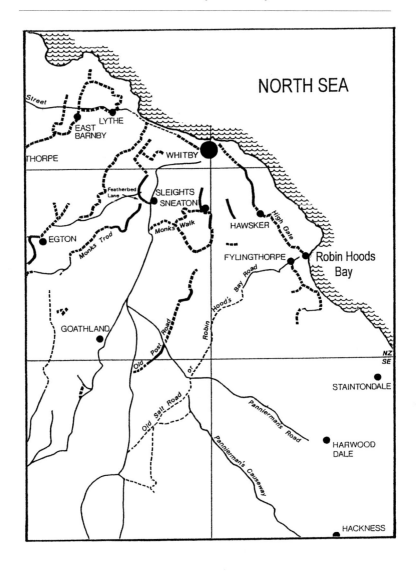

The highways around Whitby district in the 18th century.

*The rebuilt Brunswick Wesleyan Methodist Church replacing an
earlier Wesleyan Chapel and Sunday School, and situated in
Brunswick Street, which was formerly known as Scate Lane.
Now closed, it still remains a prominent landmark in the town.*

47

WHO'S WHO
IN
WHITBY HISTORY

ALAN WHITWORTH

Oscar Wilde once said, 'There is only one thing in the world worse than being talked about, and that is not being talked about. Indeed, people's fascination with private lives is the life-blood of gossip. In writing biographies and autobiographies rank high on the list of most popular books. In Whitby we have been no less fortunate in having had a select band of both the good and the bad that have helped to put this ancient seaport on the map. This work is an attempt at putting together a collection of who's who in Whitby history.

Set out in an easy alphabetical style, with cross-references leading to related entries, this is a fascinating collection of Whitby's 'worthies'.

189 PAGES : ILLUSTRATED : COLOURED FRONTIS
ISBN 1 871150 45 0

Published by Culva House Publications   **Price £8.99**

CULVA HOUSE PUBLICATIONS

A – Z of WHITBY YARDS
ALAN WHITWORTH (ISBN 1 871150 24 8)

Published in 2003 this book provides a comprehensive history of a fascinating aspect of Whitby on the Yorkshire coast. Copiously illustrated with both black and white, and coloured photos, plus line drawings and maps, it is an indispensable guide to some of the towns hidden delights.   **Price £5.99 including Postage**

TOWN HOUSE AND COUNTRY MANSIONS OF WHITBY
ALAN WHITWORTH (ISBN 1 871150 30 2)

Published 2004, this book illustrates the history and architecture of Whitby's magnificent town houses and country mansions. Hard back, easy to use gazetteer, numerous illustrations, fully indexed, 300 pages, *it comes with a CD-Rom with 300+ photos.*
Price £35.00 inc Postage

ASPECTS OF WHITBY
ALAN WHITWORTH (ISBN 1 871150 26 4)

Published for Christmas 2003, this is a new concept for Culva House Publications, a **CD-Rom** with over 400 alphabetical entries of text and over 200 photographs on every aspect of Whitby's history, which compliments the highly successful *A-Z of Whitby History.*   **Price £9.99 including Postage**

All titles can be had from **Culva House Publications, 10 The Carrs, Sleights, Whitby YO21 1RR, North Yorkshire.**
Trade enquiries welcome from bookshops & book dealers.
Telephone **01947 810819**   email **alan@culvahouse.co.uk**

See our Website at www.culvahouse.co.uk